Book 2

Teach Your Child To Play Guitar

Ages 5 and Up

The Easiest Guitar Method Ever!

Nathaniel Gunod

L. C. Harnsberger

Ron Manus

D1608290

Alfred Music
P.O. Box 10003
Van Nuys, CA 91410-0003
alfred.com

ISBN-10: 1-4706-1690-4 (Book & CD)
ISBN-13: 978-1-4706-1690-8 (Book & CD)

Cover and interior illustrations by Jeff Shelly.

 Alfred Cares. Contents printed on environmentally responsible paper.

To the Parents

Playing music on the guitar is a joyous and fulfilling activity. Sharing your love of music and the guitar is a wonderful gift that will stay with your child for a lifetime.

This volume picks up where Book 1 in the *Teach Your Child to Play Guitar* series left off. It proceeds in the same manner, with Parents Guide pages on the left and lessons for your child on the right. It begins with the 4th string, as the 1st, 2nd, and 3rd strings were covered in Book 1.

As with Book 1, an accompanying recording has demonstrations of all the examples and songs, so your child can hear how the music should sound. Also, this book includes several duets, and both parts of each duet are included separately on the recording, so your child can play along.

Parents should set aside a regular lesson time each week for the child and try to stay with this schedule. It's even a good idea to include some role playing: have your child go outside and ring the doorbell, then invite them in to begin the lessons. This will ensure that your student knows that the lessons are a special time that is separate from other activities.

This series is designed to help even parents with little-to-no music or guitar background teach their children guitar effectively. Eventually, however, it will be necessary to find an expert guitar instructor in your community. When the musical concepts or technical skills required are beyond a level that the parent can easily absorb and share, or if the lessons are creating any tension in the household, it's time to find that guitar teacher.

It's wonderful that you are involving your child in music! It will pay off in so many ways. There is much anecdotal and even scientific information to support the idea that children benefit from learning music. Take your time, encourage your child, and praise their successes. Learning to play music should be a process of moving from success to success, slowly but surely building a strong musical foundation.

Enjoy!

Contents

Notes on the Fourth String: Introducing D

In *Teach Your Child to Play Guitar, Book 1*, your child learned the notes on the 1st, 2nd, and 3rd strings. Now, it's time for your child to learn notes on the fourth string. This is an excellent time to review how to hold a pick, which is covered at the top of page 13 of Book 1. Make sure your child is holding it firmly but not squeezing too hard, and that just a small portion of the pick is sticking out below the thumb and index finger. We only use the very tip of the pick to strike a single string. Also, reinforce good left-hand technique by reminding your child to use just the tips of the fingers to press the strings directly next to the frets.

Introducing the Page

1. Review the information at the top of the page, pointing out that the D note sits on the space directly below the bottom line of the staff, which is the E note.

2. Point out the circle (O) above the note head. This means to pluck the *open* string, which is a string that is not being fingered with the left hand.

3. Direct your child to the fretboard diagram at the top right of the page; point out how strings that are not being played are represented with dotted lines, and the string being played is a solid line.

4. Practice small down strokes (toward the floor) with the pick on the fourth string.

5. Counting aloud slowly, demonstrate "Four Open Strings."

6. Have your child play along with you, as they count aloud.

7. Counting aloud slowly, demonstrate "I Choose Guitar."

8. Have your child play along with you, as they count aloud.

Practice Suggestions

1. Remember, it's always a good idea to count off one complete measure before you or your child begin to play. This sets the pace and lets them know when to begin playing. Remind them you'll say "1 2 3 4" and then they should start playing on the next "1." Demonstrate.

2. Just for fun, try saying the lyrics of the song, shown below the staff, in rhythm with your child while they play.

Subsequent Lessons

Review good practice habits with your child often. They should remember to always look over the music carefully before they play, noting the time signature, saying the names of the notes, counting and clapping the rhythms, taking special note of rests, identifying any potential tricky spots, etc. The more thorough and careful the practice sessions, the quicker we learn to play and the more fun we have!

Notes on the Fourth String
Introducing D

A note on the space below the staff is called D. You already know D on the 2nd string. This D is on the 4th string and sounds lower than D on the 2nd string. To play this note, pick the open 4th string.

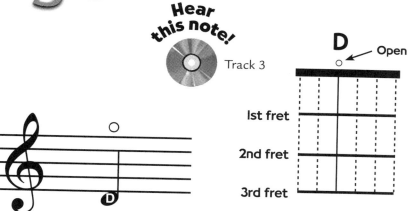

Hear this note! Track 3

D — Open

1st fret
2nd fret
3rd fret

Track 4

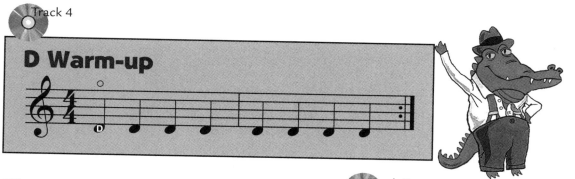

D Warm-up

Four Open Strings
Track 5

D string, new string, then three old strings: D, G, B, E. Now, that's ea - sy!

I Choose Guitar
Track 6

Trum - pets, cel - los and the flute are ve - ry nice to lis - ten to,

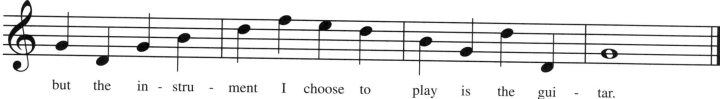

but the in - stru - ment I choose to play is the gui - tar.

*A finger number is now only shown the first time a note appears in a tune.

5

Introducing the Half-Note Slash

So far, your child has only strummed quarter notes—one beat per strum. The diamond-shaped *half-note slash* shown at the top of page 7 indicates a half-note strum—two beats per strum.

Introducing the Page

1. Review the information at the top of the page, reminding your child they learned about half notes on page 77 of Book 1. It might be a good idea to review the first two measures of "Jingle Bells" on page 78 of that book.

2. Point out that in the next song, "The Lone Star Trail," they'll be playing both strummed and picked half notes.

3. Counting aloud slowly, demonstrate "The Lone Star Trail."

4. Have your child play along with you, as they count aloud.

Practice Suggestions

Point out that the first three lines of "The Lone Start Trail" have only one fingered note: high D at the 3rd fret of the 2nd string. All the rest of the notes are played on open strings. On the fourth line, however, the 1st and 2nd fingers play C on the 2nd string and A on the 3rd string. It's a good idea to master the last four measures before playing the whole song.

Subsequent Lessons

Remember the technique of additive practice you learned on page 68 of *Teach Your Child to Play Guitar, Book 1*. This is the quickest way to learn a new song. Always remind your child that SLOW AND STEADY WINS THE RACE!

Notes:

The Lone Star Trail

Track 7

G

I start - ed on the trail on June twen - ty -

third. I been punch - in' Tex - as cat - tle on the Lone Star

Trail, sing - in', "Ki - yi yip - pi yap - pi yay, yap - pi

yay!" Sing-in', "Ki - yi yip - pi yap - pi yay!"—

G

7

Introducing Four-String Chords

All the chords your child has played thus far (C, G, G7, and D7) have been three-string chords. Now that we are playing notes on the 4th string, we can begin learning four-string versions of these and other chords.

Introducing the Page

Together with your child, look at the diagrams and photos for the G and G7 chords on page 9. Point out that to your child that the chord fingerings are identical to the G and G7 chords they already know. You only need to strum one more string! Observe that the chords now have a more full sound.

Practice Suggestions

1. Try playing each chord several times, beginning by placing the pick firmly on the 4th string and then strumming down across the top four strings in one smooth, direct strum. Listen to the chords being strummed on the recording.

2. Look through the "New Chord Exercise" at the bottom of the page making note of the half-note strums and the quarter rests in measures 4 and 8.

3. Counting aloud slowly, demonstrate the song for your child.

4. Have him or her play along with you.

5. Ask your child to count aloud and play through the song alone.

Subsequent Lessons

Looking through a new song, observing important features such as new chords or rests, before playing it for the first time is a very important aspect of efficient practice. Ensure that this part of your child's regular practice routine!

Notes:

Introducing Four-String Chords

Now that you have learned the note D on the D string, you can add it to chords you already know to make four-string versions of those chords.

Hear this chord! Track 8

The Four-String G Chord

This is the same as the three-string G chord, but you also strum the open D string.

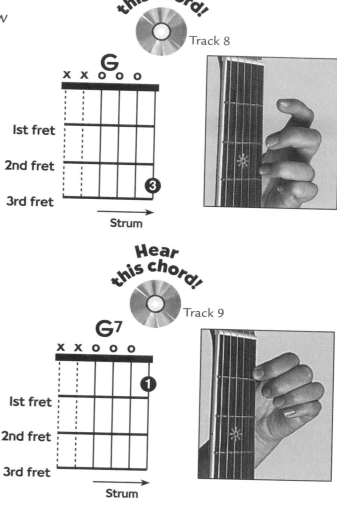

Hear this chord! Track 9

The Four-String G⁷ Chord

This is the same as the three-string G^7 chord, but you also strum the open D string.

New Chord Exercise

For this exercise, use the four-note G and G^7 chords, and also use the three-string C chord. A chord frame will be shown only the first time a chord is used. Play the chord the same way any time you see its symbol in the music again.

Track 10

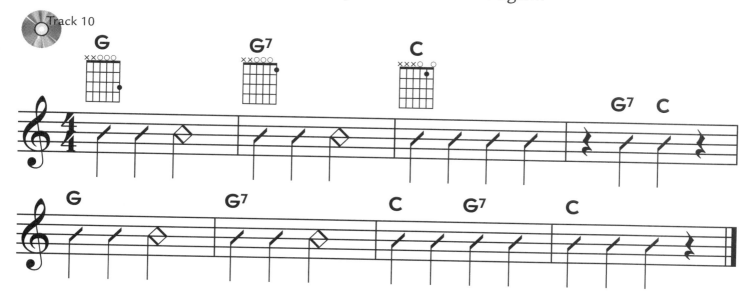

Rock Me, Mozart

"Rock Me, Mozart" uses the two four-string chords covered in the last lesson, plus the three-string C chord. It also mixes quarter notes, quarter rests, and half notes.

Introducing the Page

Together with your child, look through the song making note of the strums, picked notes, and rests. Note that the last line begins like measures 2, 3, and 4 of the first line, and that line four is the same as line three. Most good songs include lots of repeated material, which is one important reason they're easy to remember.

Practice Suggestions

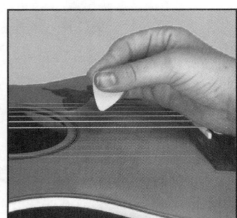

1. Practice the first two measures using the rest technique that was introduced on page 21 of *Teach Your Child to Play Guitar, Book 1*. Stop the sound of the strings by lightly touching them with the side of your hand, as in the photo.

2. Listen to Track 11 on the recording before practicing.

3. Use additive practice, learning just two measures at a time: learn two, then the next two; practice all four, then learn two more and practice all six, and so on.

Subsequent Lessons

As you child learns new concepts and techniques, it is important to review those they have already learned. It's a good idea to devote the first few minutes of each practice session to reviewing old material, and it's FUN and builds confidence! Open up Book 1 and play through one of the songs they learned previously. You'll both enjoy the activity.

Notes:

Rock Me, Mozart

Notes on the Fourth String: Introducing E

"Rock Me, Mozart" uses the two four-string chords covered in the last lesson, plus the three-string C chord. It also mixes quarter notes, quarter rests, and half notes.

Introducing the Page

1. Review the information at the top of the page, pointing out that the E note sits on the bottom line of the staff, directly above the D note.

2. Point out the "2" above the note head. This note is played with the 2nd finger.

3. Practice the E Warm-up in the middle of the page.

4. Counting aloud slowly, demonstrate "On My Horse."

5. Have your child play along with you, as they count aloud.

Practice Suggestions

1. Recognizing patterns in melodies and fingerings makes learning to play songs easier. For example, in "On My Horse," the quarter-, quarter-, half-note pattern (♩♩ ♩) found in measures one and two, and the half-, quarter-, quarter-note pattern (♩ ♩♩) found in measures three and four, are very important features of the melody. Together with your child, count the number of times that two quarter notes and a half note appear in a measure together.

2. You should have found eight measures that include two quarter notes and a half note in this song. Noticing them will make it easier to learn!

3. Now, notice the fingering/string pattern in the third measure of the first line: open on the 2nd string, then down to 2nd, open, 2nd on the the 3rd string. Then look at the fingering pattern in the next-to-last measure of the song: open on the 3rd string, then down to the 2nd finger, open, 2nd finger on the 4th string. It's the same fingering/string pattern! Knowing this makes the song easier to learn.

Subsequent Lessons

Recognizing patterns in melodies and fingerings is a very important part of why learning music is so helpful to your child's mental development. Keep this in mind as you explore new songs together with your child.

Notes:

Notes on the Fourth String
Introducing E

A note on the lowest line of the staff is called E. You already know E that is the open 1st string. This E is on the 4th string and sounds lower. To play this note, use finger 2 to press the 4th string at the 2nd fret. Pick only the 4th string.

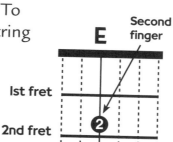

Hear this note!
Track 12

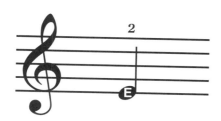

Track 13

E Warm-up

Track 14

On My Horse

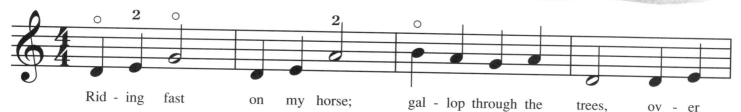

Rid - ing   fast   on   my   horse;   gal - lop through the   trees,   ov - er

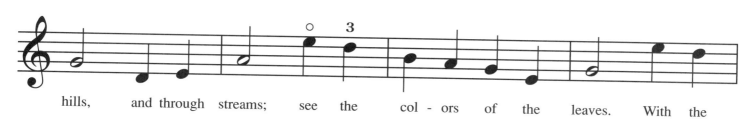

hills,   and through   streams;   see   the   col - ors   of   the   leaves.   With the

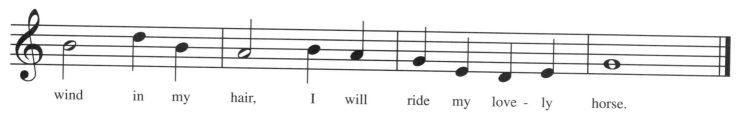

wind   in   my   hair,   I   will   ride   my   love - ly   horse.

Old MacDonald Had a Farm, The Four-String C Chord, Introducing Common Time, and C Blues

"Old MacDonald Had a Farm" will provide more practice on the 4th-string E note and the four-string G chord. "C Blues" includes the four-string C chord.

Introducing the Page

1. Review the four-string C chord with your child, pointing out that the top three strings are the same as for the three-string C chord; we just add the 4th-string E note to the bottom to create a four-string chord. Both the 1st and 2nd finger are used to play the chord. It's important to make sure neither finger is bumping into an adjacent string; all four strings must ring out clearly so help your child use just the tips of their fingers to play the chord.

2. Review the $\frac{4}{4}$ time signature, which was introcued on page 15 of Book 1. Explain how it is sometimes written with a ℃, and we also call this time signature "common time."

Practice Suggestions

1. Can your child find the important rhythm pattern in "Old MacDonald Had a Farm?" If they said six quarters and a half note (♩♩♩♩♩♩ 𝅗𝅥), they were correct. This pattern comprises almost the whole song!

2. Point out that the second line is almost identical to the first line.

3. In "C Blues," point out that the melody in measure 1 is repeated in measures 3, 7, and 11.

4. Counting aloud slowly, demonstrate "C Blues" before inviting your child to play along with you.

Subsequent Lessons

Encourage slow additive practice. Confident, accurate playing will never arise from confusion and error.

Notes:

Old MacDonald Had a Farm

Track 15

G

Old Mac-Don-ald   had   a   farm,   E - I - E - I - O!   And

on that farm he   had gui - tars!   E - I - E - I - O!

G

The Four-String C Chord

This chord is the same as the three-string C chord, but you also put finger 2 on the 2nd fret of the 4th string.

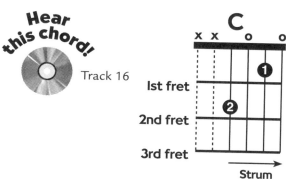

Hear this chord!   Track 16

Introducing Common Time 𝄴

This symbol is a time signature that means the same as $\frac{4}{4}$.

$𝄴 = \frac{4}{4}$ The 4 on the top means there are 4 beats in each measure.
The 4 on the bottom means a quarter note gets 1 beat.

C Blues   Track 17

Use the four-string C chord.

15

Notes on the Fourth String: Introducing F

The F note is written on the bottom space of the staff and is played with the 3rd finger at the 3rd fret of the 4th string. "Baseball" will provide practice with the F note and the four-string G7 chord.

Introducing the Page

1. Review the information at the top of the page, pointing out that the F note sits on the bottom space of the staff.

2. Point out the 3 above the note head. This note is played with the 3rd finger. Make note of the photograph showing the tip of the finger placed directly next to the fret.

3. Play the "F Warm-up" together.

4. Counting aloud slowly, demonstrate "Baseball."

5. Have your child play along with you as they count aloud.

Practice Suggestions

1. This song has lots of slow-moving half notes so you may be able to learn it four measures at a time instead of the usual two measures at a time.

2. Just for fun, try saying the lyrics of the song, shown below the staff, in rhythm with your child while they play.

Notes:

Notes on the Fourth String
Introducing F

A note on the lowest space of the staff is called F. You already know F on the 1st string. This F is on the 4th string and sounds lower than F on the 1st string. To play this note, use finger 3 to press the 4th string at the 3rd fret. Pick only the 4th string.

Hear this note!
Track 18

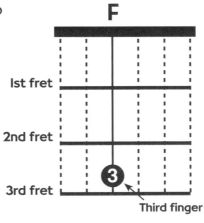

F

1st fret

2nd fret

3rd fret

3 Third finger

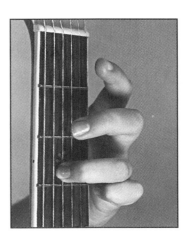

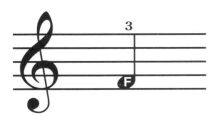

Track 19

F Warm-up

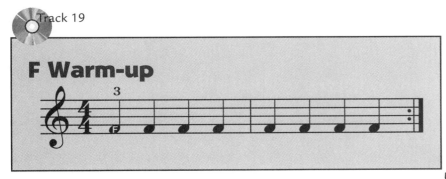

Baseball

Remember to use the four-string G⁷ chord.

Track 20

G⁷
xx○○○

Knuck - le ball, curve ball, fast ball, strike!

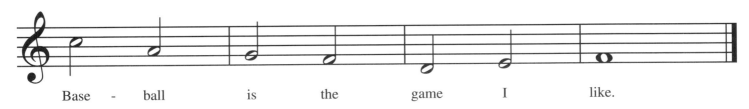

Base - ball is the game I like.

Reuben, Reuben

"Reuben, Reuben" will provide more practice for the 4th-string F note, and the four-string C chord.

Introducing the Page

1. Point out that the second half of the piece is exactly the same as the first half. In other words, the melody of the first eight measures is repeated with different words.

2. Also, measures 3 and 4 are almost identical to measures 1 and 2. A four-sting C chord punctuates the end of the line. This is also true of the third line.

Practice Suggestions

1. Using additive practice, this will be a fun and easy song to learn.

2. Once your child has mastered the first eight measures, they are ready to play the whole song!

3. It will be fun for your child to sing the silly words while playing this song.

Notes:

Reuben, Reuben

Remember to use the four-string C chord.

Track 21

Reu - ben, Reu - ben, I've been think - ing what a weird world this would be

if the mon - keys lived in hous - es and we swung from tree to tree.

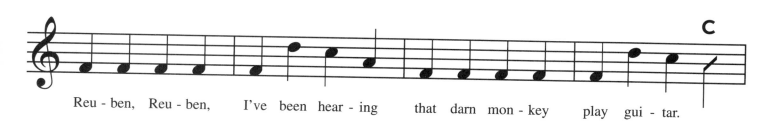

Reu - ben, Reu - ben, I've been hear - ing that darn mon - key play gui - tar.

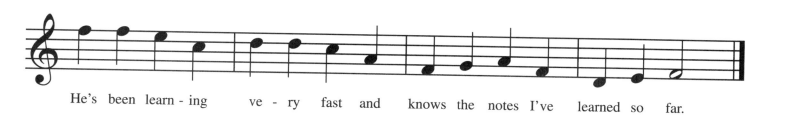

He's been learn - ing ve - ry fast and knows the notes I've learned so far.

Dotted Half Notes & $\frac{3}{4}$ Time

In $\frac{3}{4}$ time, sometimes called *waltz time*, there are three equal beats in each measure. As always, the 4 on the bottom of the time signature means a quarter note gets one beat.

Introducing the Page

1. Remind your child that the time signature tells us how many beats are in each measure, and point out the 3 in this new time signature.

2. Draw his or her attention to the dotted half note lesson, and explain that adding a dot to the right of a half note adds an additional beat, changing it from a two-beat note to a three-beat note.

3. Show him or her how the note values in the $\frac{3}{4}$ example add up to three beats in each measure.

4. Together with your child, count aloud "1, 2, 3, 1, 2, 3," etc. and clap through the "Clap and Count out Loud" exercise. Remember to hold your hands together during the half note and dotted half notes.

Practice Suggestions

1. Notice that measure 2 in "Three Is for Me!" is identical to measure 1, and measure 6 is identical to measure 5.

2. Encourage your child to emphasize beat 1 in each measure by playing it just a little louder, and discuss how this time signature "feels" different than $\frac{4}{4}$.

3. Use slow, careful additive practice until it is easy to play through the whole song at a moderate pace.

Subsequent Lessons

From now, checking the time signature should be part of preparing to play every song or exercise. It could be $\frac{4}{4}$, or it could be $\frac{3}{4}$!

Notes:

Dotted Half Notes & 3/4 Time

The 3/4 Time Signature

Introducing the Dotted Half Note

3 beats

This note looks like a half note, but with a dot to the right of the notehead. It lasts three beats.

A 3/4 time signature ("three-four time") means there are 3 equal beats in every measure.

3/4

The 3 on the top means there are 3 beats in each measure.

The 4 on the bottom means a quarter note gets 1 beat.

Track 22

Clap and Count out Loud

Count: 1 2 3   1 2 3   1 2 3   1 2 3

Three Is for Me!

Track 23

One, two, three. One, two, three. Three is for me!

Play - ing in three with the great - est of ease.

21

Daisy Bell

This song includes playing two notes at the same time, which is called a *double stop*.

Introducing the Page

1. Together with your child, point to every spot in the music for "Daisy Bell" where two notes are stacked, one on top of the other. You should find 15 double stops.

2. Explain that to play two notes at the same time, it is best to think of the two adjacent strings as being one, great big, fat string, and the pick should move directly and quickly across them both—but *just those two strings*. It should be a little flick of the wrist, so the pick moves up and away from the next, third string. The two strings should sound as if they were struck simultaneously...you should hear one, sweet sound.

3. Point out that most of the double stops have one open string, except for the one that is used three times in measures 5, 6, and 21. It uses two fingers (3 and 2).

4. Point out the ⅜ time signature.

5. Point out the strummed chords in the last three lines. There are quarter-note and half-note strums. The chords are four-string G7, G, and C.

6. Observe the difference between picking a double stop and strumming a chord; these are two, very different right-hand techniques.

Practice Suggestions

1. Find every double stop in the song and practice it several times, until it is secure. Plan to spend the most time with the two-finger double stop used in measures 5, 6, and 21. These are all the same.

2. After learning all of the double stops, use additive practice to master the rest of the song.

3. When a measure starts with a half note and finishes with a quarter note, the quarter note usually "leads" into the next measure. It is a good idea to practice going from beat 3 into beat 1 of the next measure, so the two measures are smoothly connected.

Subsequent Lessons

Looking for stacked notes (double stops) in the music should become part of your child's preparations for learning every new song or exercise, along with observing other details about the music, such as the time signature, rests, where there are strummed chords instead of picked notes, etc.

Daisy Bell

Track 24

Playing Two Notes at Once

Sometimes, two notes are played at one time. In "Daisy Bell," usually when this happens one of the notes is an open string, but there are three places where both notes are fingered.

Dai - sy,   Dai - sy,   give   me   your

an - swer,   do.   I'm   half

cra - zy   all   for   the   love   of   you.   It

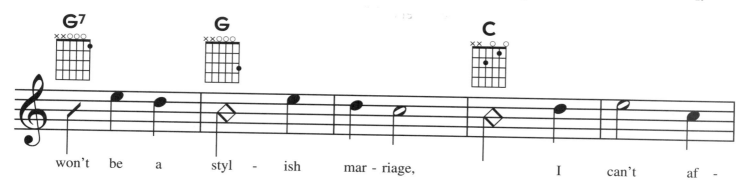

won't   be   a   styl - ish   mar - riage,   I   can't   af -

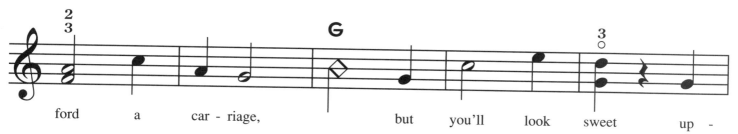

ford   a   car - riage,   but   you'll   look   sweet   up -

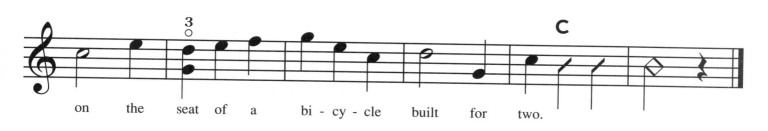

on   the   seat   of   a   bi - cy - cle   built   for   two.

Notes on the Fifth String: Introducing A

The low, 5th-string A is played on the open string and is written on the second of two *ledger lines*, which extend the staff down or up.

Introducing the Page

1. Show your child the introduction to the A note on page 25, and introduce the ledger lines. This new note is easy to recognize because it has two ledger lines. Have fun together describing the note. Maybe it looks like someone with a halo, and a stick going in one ear and out the other! Let your child use his or her imagination! It will make it fun and easy to learn the new note.

2. Play the "A Warm-up" together.

3. "Five Open Strings" is easy to play because it requires just the right hand; no left-hand fingers are needed.

4. Notice that the exercises and songs on this page are in $\frac{4}{4}$.

5. Observe the rests in "Trash Truck."

6. Notice that in "Trash Truck," measures 1, 2, 5, and the first part of 7 are identical. This will make it easier to learn.

Practice Suggestions

1. Try using one slow, smooth downstroke with the pick to play measure 1 into measure 2 of "Five Open Strings." In other words, move the pick directly into the next string instead moving it away from the strings after picking the string. These are called *rest strokes*. Then try one slow, smooth upstroke with the pick to play measure 3. Isolate these measures and master them. Keep the rhythm even.

2. Be sure to mute the strings to create silences for the rests in "Trash Truck."

3. Just for fun, try saying the lyrics of the song, shown below the staff, in rhythm with your child while they play.

Notes:

Notes on the Fifth String
Introducing A

A line that extends the staff either up or down is called a *ledger line*. A note two ledger lines below the staff is called A. You already know A on the 3rd string. This A is the open 5th string and sounds lower than A on the 3rd string. To play this note, pick the open 5th string.

Hear this note!
Track 25

← Ledger lines

A ← Open

1st fret

2nd fret

3rd fret

Track 26

A Warm-up

Five Open Strings
Track 27

A D G B E, the op-en strings I'm play-ing.

Trash Truck
Track 28

Trash truck, trash truck, makes the gar-bage go.

Trash truck, trash truck, the driv-er's name is Joe.

Scarborough Fair

"Scarborough Fair" is an ancient, traditional song from Great Britain popularized in the 1960s by the renowned duo, Simon and Garfunkel.

Introducing the Page

1. Together with your child, look through the music and observe the $\frac{3}{4}$ time signature and the rest at the end.

2. Notice that some of the notes do not have lyrics below them. These are "filler" and should not be given the same emphasis as the melody notes with lyrics written below them.

3. Remember that, in $\frac{3}{4}$ time, when a measure starts with a half note and finishes with a quarter note, the quarter note should smoothly connect to the next measure.

Practice Suggestions

1. Find every measure that begins with a half note and finishes with a quarter note. Practice smoothly connecting each of those measures to the measures that follow them, as in additive practice. For example, practice going from measure 1 to measure 2, then measure 2 to measure 3, which is a little trickier because the same finger is used twice in a row. It's always easier to smoothly connect two notes played with different fingers.

Subsequent Lessons

It's always fun to learn about the origins of old folk songs, and to listen to different recordings of them. Your child will enjoy hearing Simon and Garfunkel sing a song they can play!

Notes:

Scarborough Fair

Track 29

Are you goin' to Scar - bor - ough Fair?

Pars - ley, sage, rose - ma - ry and

thyme. Re - mem - ber me to

one who lives there, _____ she once

was a true love of mine.

Notes on the Fifth String: Introducing B

The low, 5th-string B is played on the 2nd fret with the 2nd finger, and is written just below the first ledger line below the staff.

Introducing the Page

1. Show your child the introduction to the B note on page 29. This new note is easy to recognize because it sits just below one ledger line. Maybe it looks like the note is wearing a hat! Again, asking your child to use his or her imagination to come up with a silly description for the note will make learning it more fun and easy.

2. Play the "B Warm-up" together.

3. Notice that measures 1, 3, and 5 of "Cleaning Up" are identical.

4. Pay attention to where there is a change from picked notes to strummed chords, and back to picked notes, such as in measures 2 to 3.

Practice Suggestions

1. Measures 1, 3, and 5 of "Cleaning Up" include a lot of *string skipping*, going from the 3rd, to the 2nd, to the 4th, and back to the 3rd. Measure 7 skips from the 2nd to the 5th string and back. Isolate these measures and master them before playing through the whole song.

2. Additive practice will help ensure that the spots with string skipping, or changes from picked notes to strums and back, get adequate attention.

Subsequent Lessons

Make sure your child is always looking for potential technical challenges in the music before beginning to practice a song or exercise.

Notes:

Notes on the Fifth String
Introducing B

A note on the space one ledger line below the staff is called B. You already know B that is the open 2nd string. This B is on the 5th string and sounds lower than B on the 2nd string. To play this note, use finger 2 to press the 5th string at the 2nd fret. Pick only the 5th string.

Hear this note!
Track 30

B   Second finger

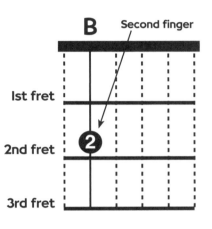

1st fret
2nd fret
3rd fret

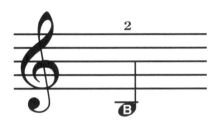

Track 31

B Warm-up

Cleaning Up
Track 32

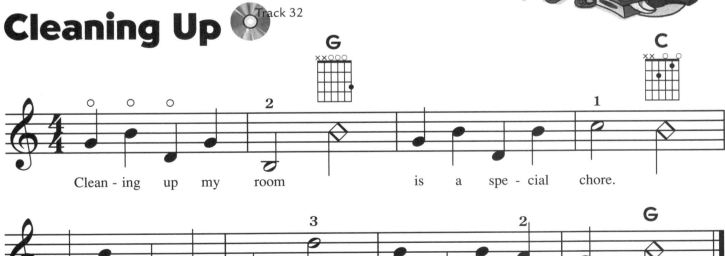

G   C

Clean - ing up my room   is a spe - cial chore.

If I don't get done, I can't op - en my door!

29

My Pet Cat

"My Pet Cat" provides a chance to practice using the low A and B notes on the fifth string combined with lots of notes on other strings. It is also another great example of a song where pattern recognition makes learning easier.

Introducing the Page

1. Together with your child, observe the fingerings in the first measure: o 2 o 2, first on the 5th string, and then on the 4th string. The second measure is the same as the first, and then the third measure also begins with the o 2 fingerings. This easy fingering pattern is repeated throughout the song. The fourth measure begins the same way.

2. Almost every fingered note in "My Pet Cat" is followed by an open string. The only exception is the note A in the third measure, which is played with the 2nd finger and followed by a C played with the 1st finger on the 1st fret of the 2nd string. The seventh measure is the same. Give these measures some extra practice.

3. Notice that the second line of music is almost identical to the first line.

Practice Suggestions

1. Once the first line is mastered, the second line is just about mastered, too! Just make sure the fourth measure of the second line gets some attention, since it is different than the fourth measure of the the first line.

Subsequent Lessons

Looking for fingering patterns always helps to make a song or exercise easier to play!

Notes:

My Pet Cat

Track 33

Run - ning af - ter my pet cat and my pet cat will chase a rat. And

once that rat runs in its hole, I'll catch my cat and that's my goal.

"Meow meow meow meow, meow meow meow meow, meow meow meow meow, meow meow." Crash!

Notes on the Fifth String: Introducing C

The low, 5th-string C is played on the 3rd fret with the 3rd finger, and is written on the first ledger line below the staff.

Introducing the Page

1. Show your child the introduction to the C note on page 33. This new note is easy to recognize because it sits on the first ledger line. Ask your child what it looks like. Maybe it looks like a note with big ears!

2. Play the "C Warm-up" together.

3. Notice that measures 1 and 2 of "Barking Song" are identical. Measures 5 and 6 are very similar, too. One note is different. Ask your child to find the different note in measure 6 (it's the fourth beat of measure 6, which is D instead of F).

4. Pay attention to the rests, and where there is a change from picked notes to strummed chords in measures 4 and 8.

Practice Suggestions

1. This song uses notes on the 5th, 4th, and 3rd strings. It would be a good idea to ask your child to point at each note and say which string it is on (like this: 5-4-4-5-4-4-5-4-4-4-4-strum-strum, 4-4-4-4-4-4-4-4-3-4-4-4-5-strum-strum).

2. Use additive practice, learning two measures at a time and then adding them to the previous measures.

3. "Barking Song" has fun lyrics. Your child will enjoy playing the notes as you sing along.

Subsequent Lessons

Make reciting the string numbers part of every practice session that includes learning a new song.

Notes:

Notes on the Fifth String
Introducing C

A note one ledger line below the staff is called C. You already know C on the 2nd string. This C is on the 5th string and sounds lower than C on the 2nd string. To play this note, use finger 3 to press the 5th string at the 3rd fret. Pick only the 5th string.

Hear this note!
Track 34

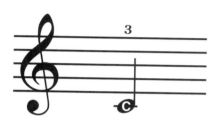

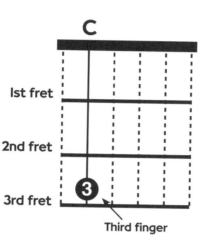

C

1st fret

2nd fret

3rd fret ③

Third finger

Track 35

C Warm-up

Barking Song

Track 36

G

3 ○ 2   3

"Woof, woof, woof!   Woof, woof, woof!"   says Bel - la, my   dog.

C

She will bark both   day and night, and   e - ven in the   fog.

33

Volga Boatmen and Peter Gray

"Volga Boatmen" is a well-known traditional Russian song which was sung by *burlaks*, or barge-haulers, on the Volga River. "Peter Gray" is a traditional American ballad about a young man whose fiancee is sent out west after her father discovers their plan to get married. The man goes west to find her.

Introducing the Page

1. "Volga Boatmen" is played entirely on the 4th and 5th strings. The note pattern C–A–D–D–A occurs several times, once with only one D note. Together with your child, find all three occurences (measures 1 and 2, 3 and 4, and 7 and 8). Point these out to your child. As always, noticing patterns such as these makes it easier to learn a new song.

2. After your child has learned "Volga Boatmen," go on to "Peter Gray." The important note pattern in this song is less obvious, but it is there, and noting it will be helpful: up three notes and down one. You'll see this in measures 1 (low A–B–C–B), 3 (C–D–E–D), and 5 (high A–B–C–B). Point these out to your child.

Practice Suggestions

1. In general, it's a good idea to keep left-hand fingers down while ascending a string. For example, in measure 1 of "Peter Gray," your child should keep the 2nd finger down on the B while adding the 3rd finger to play the C. This makes for a smoother connection between the notes and, in this case, the music calls for the B note with the 2nd finger on the next beat.

2. Notice that in measure 4 of "Peter Gray," your child will be playing a half note on the second beat. This is the first time they have played this rhythm! Be sure to cout out loud and clap the rhythm in this measure with your child.

Subsequent Lessons

By now, your child has a number of important practice strategies to apply when learning a new song. Some of them were introduced in Book 1. Here's a quick review:

1. Point at each note and say its letter name.
2. Point at each note and say which string it's on (1, 2, 3, 4, or 5).
3. Count aloud and clap the rhythms, holding the hands together during longer notes and taking them apart for rests.
4. Look through the piece and identify special features, such as chord strums, rests, big string skips, and note patterns.
5. Additive practice: learn to play a small portion, such as one or two measures, then learn to play the next portion, then learn to play those two portions together, then learn the next portion, add that to the previous two, and so on.

Volga Boatmen

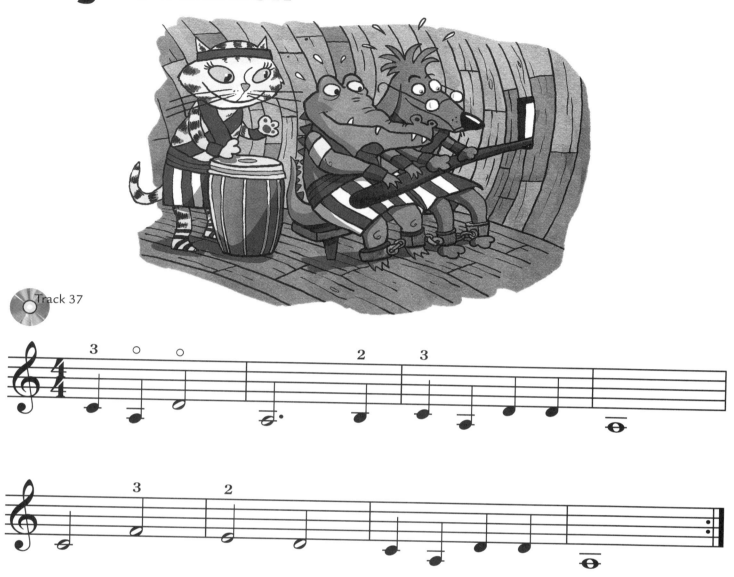

Track 37

Peter Gray

Track 38

Liebesträum and Introducing the Dotted-Half-Note Slash

"Liebesträum" was written in 1845 by the famous composer Franz Liszt. The title means "love dream."

Introducing the Page

1. Introduce the dotted-half-note slash. It is the same length as the dotted half note learned on page 21.

2. Together with your child, find all of the dotted half notes and slashes in the song "Liebesträum." You should find 15 (12 notes and 3 slashes).

3. Point out the repeat sign at the end of measure 12 and remind your child that this means to go back to the beginning and play the first part of the song a second time, then continue past the repeat. The repeat sign was introduced on page 35 of Book 1.

4. As you look through the piece with your child to identify its special features, notice the ¾ time signature and two places where two notes are played at the same time (double stops) in measures 4 and 24.

5. Also point out that the last 12 measures of the song are identical to the first 12 measures, except for the A note in measure.

6. The first seven measures of the song are mostly just the E note on the 4th string at the 2nd fret, with one two-note strum and one F-note inserted.

Practice Suggestions

1. To insert the double stop on the first beat of measure 4, and then return to the E-note after it requires careful string skipping. Before practicing the song, have your child make those two measures into an exercise and repeat it many times, at first watching the right hand closely and then trying to play without watching.

2. Returning to the C note after strumming the four-string C chord in measure 16 also requires careful string skipping. Measure 16 should also be mastered before trying to practice the whole song.

Notes:

Liebesträum

This song was written in 1845 by the famous composer Franz Liszt. The title means "love dream."

Introducing the Dotted-Half-Note Slash

The dotted-half-note slash is the same length as a dotted half note.

3 beats

Track 39

A Minor Boogies

"A Minor Boogie" is a fun song that will provide additional practice playing on the 5th, 4th, 3rd, 2nd, and 1st strings.

Introducing the Page

1. The special features you should note in this song are the quarter rests, the repeat sign at the end of measure 8, the two notes played together at the very end, and the recurring melodic *phrases*. A phrase is a complete musical thought. For example, the first phrase is measures 1 through 4. The second phrase, beginning in measure 5, starts exactly like the first, but ends differently. They are *parallel phrases* and noticing their similarities will make them easier to learn.

2. Notice that the last eight measures are identical to the first eight except for the last two measures, which close the piece.

3. The second and third phrases, measures 9 through 16, are also parallel phrases. Makse sure you child observes the differences between the ends of the two phrases.

Practice Suggestions

1. As always, your child should be very thorough in preparing to play. He or she should make sure they know all the note names, which strings they are on, and also be very clear about the rhythm and where there are rests.

2. He or she should use additive practice, playing slowly and carefully until confident.

Notes:

A Minor Boogie

Track 40

Notes on the Sixth String: Introducing E

The lowest E is played on the open 6th string, and is written below the third ledger line below the staff.

Introducing the Page

1. Show your child the introduction to the E note on page 41. This new note is easy to recognize because it sits below the third ledger line. Ask your child what it looks like. Maybe it looks a note wearing three hats!

2. Play the "E Warm-up" together.

3. "Six Open Strings," which is in $\frac{3}{4}$ time, uses every string on the guitar and starts with a simple pattern: play up three strings, and down one. In measure 5, the pattern changes, and starting on the second beat in measure 6, all six strings are played in order, starting from the 1st string and ending on the 6th on the very last note of the song.

4. Notice that "Giraffe Under the Staff" is in $\frac{3}{4}$ time and has either two notes together or a chord at the end of every four-measure phrase.

Practice Suggestions

1. Make sure your child can point at every note and say its name and which string it's on. For example, "Six Open Strings" is: E-6, A-5, D-4, A-5, etc. Use additive practice, learning two measures at a time and then adding them to the previous measures.

2. He or she should do the same thing for "Giraffe Under the Staff," but include the fret numbers. For example, the song starts like this: A-5-open; C-5-3rd fret; B-5-2nd fret; A-5-open, etc. The more one knows about a song before playing, the easier it is to learn!

3. Your child should practice each change from single notes to two notes played together (or a chord), and then back to single notes, as an exercise before working through the piece with additive practice.

Notes:

Notes on the Sixth String
Introducing E

Hear this note! Track 41

A note on the space under the third ledger line below the staff is called E. This E is on the 6th string, and it is the lowest-sounding note on the guitar. To play this note, pick the open 6th string.

E

Open
1st fret
2nd fret
3rd fret

Track 42

E Warm-up

Six Open Strings
Track 43

Now   we   have   learned   six   op - en   strings.

From   high   to   low: E   B   G   D   A   E.

Giraffe Under the Staff
Track 44

Three   lines   be - low   the   staff   hides   a   big,

tall   gir - affe!   Be   care - ful   if   you

find   him,   be - cause   you   just   might   laugh!

Two E's

"Two E's" has two spots where your child will get to skip from the high E on the 1st string to the lowest E on the 6th string.

Introducing the Page

1. Together with your child, locate the two spots where there is a skip from high E to the lowest E. One is on the second line, third measure, and the other is in the fourth line, first measure. Your child may have to watch his or her right hand to move from the 1st string to the 6th.

2. The dotted-half-note/quarter-note rhythm ($\,$♩.$\,$ ♩$\,$) is very important in this song.

Practice Suggestions

1. Be sure to encourage your child to count and clap the rhythms before playing, making special note of the dotted-half-note/quarter-note rhythms.

2. Make an exercise of alternating between the high E on the open 1st string and the lowest E on the open 6th string, over and over again.

Notes:

Two E's

Track 45

C

There are two op - en E's on my gui -

G

tar: high E and low E. If

I use them right, I will go far. **C**

First - string E and sixth - string E will make me a big star! **C**

43

Notes on the Sixth String: Introducing F

The low F is played with finger 1 on the 6th string at the 1st fret, and is written on the third ledger line below the staff.

Introducing the Page

1. Show your child the introduction to the F note on page 45. This new note is easy to recognize because it sits directly on the third ledger line below the staff. Ask your child what it looks like. Maybe it looks like a bug climbing a ladder!

2. Play the "F Warm-up" together.

3. Inroduce your child to the *fermata*. It is sometimes called a "birds eye," or a "hold sign." It means to hold the note for extra time, usually, twice the value of the note. It is often found above the last note of a piece. Holding the last note for extra time makes it sound more final.

4. "Dad's Classic Car," ends with a half-note C chord with a fermata. A half note would ordinarily get two beats, but this one has a fermata, so it should ring for two extra beats.

5. Point out to your child that in the second line of the song, the music goes back and forth between low E and low F.

6. The first several measures can be played by placing fingers 1 and 2 in position for a four-string C chord. They can be left down on their notes all the way until it's time to play the D on the fourth beat of the fourth measure.

Practice Suggestions

1. This song has lots of different rhythms, so it is a good idea to become expert at counting and clapping the rhythm before playing.

2. It would be a good idea to play measure 3 over and over again, like an exercise. This will make going back to plucking the 4th string after strumming the four-string C chord easy.

Notes:

Notes on the Sixth String
Introducing F

Hear this note!  Track 46

A note on the third ledger line below the staff is called F. To play this note, use finger 1 to press the 6th string at the 1st fret. Pick only the 6th string.

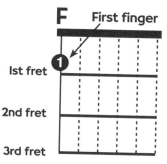

Track 47

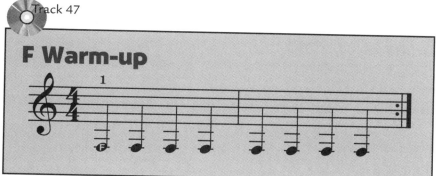

F Warm-up

Dad's Classic Car

Introducing the Fermata

This symbol is a *fermata*. It is sometimes called a "bird's eye" because it looks like the eye of a bird. When you see a fermata over or under a note, play the note a little longer than it would normally be played. You should hold it about twice as long as usual.

Track 48

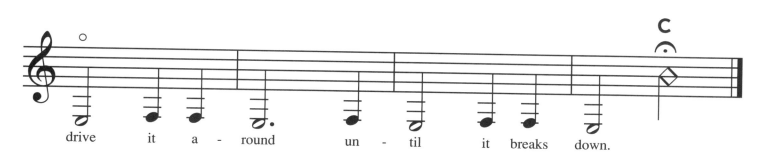

My dad's clas - sic car does - n't go far. We

drive it a - round un - til it breaks down.

Sakura

This beautiful Japanese song about Spring and cherry blossoms has been popular since the 19th century. It sounds best when played slowly.

Introducing the Page

1. The entire melody is played on the lowest three strings: the 4th, 5th, and 6th strings.

2. This haunting melody has several recurring musical ideas. The three-note melody in measure 1 is immediately repeated in measure 2. It then reappears in the second and third measures of the fourth line. Also, the melody in measures 3 and 4 returns at the beginning of the third line, and the melody in measures 5 and 6 returns at the end of the third line.

3. The song does not return to the starting note, low A on the 5th string, at the end, which adds to its exotic sound.

Practice Suggestions

1. This is a great opportunity to make sure your child can discriminate between all the low notes with ledger lines that have been covered so far. Make sure they can name the notes out loud in rhythm before playing.

2. Additive practice will make it easy for your child to learn to play this song.

Notes:

Sakura

This song is one of Japan's most beautiful folk songs. The word *sakura* literally means "cherry blossom."

 Track 49

Sa - ku - ra,　　Sa - ku - ra,　　cher - ry　blos - soms

in　the　sky,　　near　and　far　as　eye　can　see,

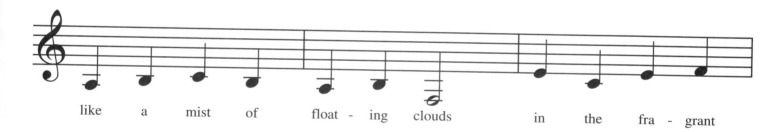

like　a　mist　of　float - ing　clouds　in　the　fra - grant

blush　of　spring.　Come,　oh　come.　Come,　oh　come.

Come　and　see　the　cher - ry　trees.

47

Notes on the Sixth String: Introducing G

The low G is played with finger 3 on the 6th string at the 3rd fret, and is written below the second ledger line below the staff.

Introducing the Page

1. Show your child the introduction to the G note on page 49. This new note is easy to recognize because it sits right below the second ledger line below the staff. Ask your child what it looks like. Maybe it looks like a silly lady balancing two dinner plates on her head!

2. Play the "G Warm-up" together.

3. The song "All the Notes I Know So Far" is exciting! It gives your child the chance to play from the lowest note on the guitar, low E on the open 6th string, all the way up to the highest note they know, high G on the 1st string at the 3rd fret.

4. "Do-Re-Mi Is for Me!" uses syllables we call *solfege*. A syllable is assigned to each note. This may remind you of a famous song from the musical, *The Sound of Music*.

5. It would be a good idea to point out that when music is getting higher-sounding, it looks like it is going higher on the page. This is one of the wonderful things about music notation—it sort of looks the way it sounds!

Practice Suggestions

1. Make sure your child can name every note, and say what string and fret it is on. For example, the first four notes of "All the Notes I Know So Far" are E, 6th open; F, 6th, 1; G, 6th, 3; A, 5th, open. Be creative and make this a fun game. Take turns and see how fast you both can go!

2. Remember, slow and steady wins the race! Encourage your child to practice carefully, without error. Practicing too fast can lead to frustration and confusion.

Subsequent Lessons

Now that your child is reading and playing 17 different notes, from the lowest E to the high G on the 1st string, it is important to help him or her use all of the best practice habits. It should *never* feel difficult or confusing to play the guitar. There is always a way to prepare, and a speed at which to play, where success is achievable. Frustration is the biggest reason students quit. Make sure they are *always* succeeding!

Notes on the Sixth String
Introducing G

 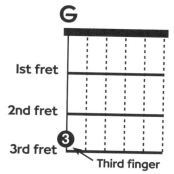

A note on the space two ledger lines below the staff is called G. Use finger 3 to press the 6th string at the 3rd fret. Pick only the 6th string.

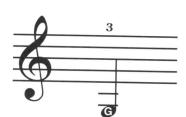

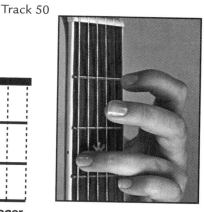

G

1st fret

2nd fret

3rd fret ③ Third finger

Track 51

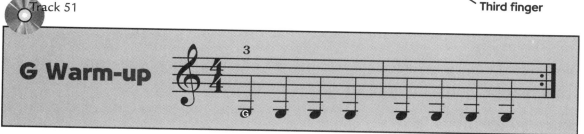

G Warm-up

All the Notes I Know So Far Track 52

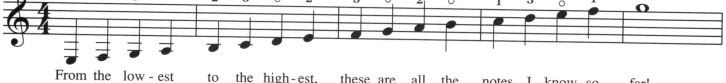

From the low-est to the high-est, these are all the notes I know so far!

From the high-est to the low-est, play-ing all the notes is real-ly fun!

Do-Re-Mi Is for Me! Track 53

Using syllables like *Do* and *Re* for notes is called *solfège* ("sol-FEZH").

Do re mi fa sol la ti do. Do re mi fa sol.

Do ti la sol fa mi. Sol fa mi re do!

Spy Rock

"Spy Rock" is a fun song that uses all six strings of the guitar.

Introducing the Page

1. The main feature of this melody is a melodic pattern found in the first measure: E–G–A–B. It occurs several times during the song.

2. Most of the melody is characterized by this pattern of open strings and fretted notes: open–fretted–open–fretted. This makes the melody easy and fun to play. Plus, it makes it easy to learn quickly. Help your child find the three places in the melody where this pattern is broken (hint: measure 3, where the pattern is reveresed; measure 7, first and second beats; and the last measure, which has two open E notes).

3. Your child will only need two left-hand fingers to play this song: 2 and 3. This is another reason it is an easy song to learn.

Practice Suggestions

1. This song will reinforce your child's knowledge of the notes written with ledger lines below the staff. Make sure they can recite the names of the notes in an even steady rhythm before attempting to play.

2. Then, make sure your child can also name the fret and string number for each note in the section they are about to practice. For example, before playing the first two measures, they should be able to recite "open 6th, 3rd fret 5th, open 5th, 2nd fret 5th," etc. It's great to combine these elements and recite the note names, frets, and strings together, like "E, open, 6th; G, 3rd, 6th," etc.

3. As always, slow and steady wins the race, and additive practice is the best method for learing a song quickly.

Notes:

Spy Rock

Track 54

I'm a spy for just the good guys, catch-ing bad guys right and left,

sec-ret gad-gets in my pock-ets, find-ing crooks be-fore a theft.

Bad guys run when they see me, I walk up and then they flee!

I'm a spy for you, now don't you want to be like me?

The Farmer in the Dell

This popular children's song probably came to America with immigrants from Germany in the 19th century. It is popular in various versions all over the world.

Introducing the Page

1. This song combines strumming the four-string C chord with plucked notes on the 6th, 5th, 4th, and 3rd strings.

2. The melody includes a lot of repeated notes, which makes it easy to learn and play.

3. The main notes of the melody are C, E, and G, which happen to be the notes used to create the C chord.

4. The time signature is $\frac{3}{4}$, and the half-note/quarter-note rhythm (♩ ♪) is an important feature.

Practice Suggestions

1. Before playing, work on the rhythm. Together with your child, count aloud "1, 2, 3, 1, 2, 3," etc., and clap the rhythm. Then, try tapping your feet and singing the melody with the words.

2. Your child will have fun learning more about the songs they play. There are at least nine more verses to this song; look for them below!

3. There is a fun circle game that is sometimes played while singing this song. Children (10 or more) join hands and dance in a circle going around the farmer who stands in the center. At the end of the first verse, the farmer chooses a wife and she joins him inside the circle. After the second verse, the wife takes a child. This continues until the last verse when everyone is in the circle except the cheese. Next time, the cheese gets to be the farmer. Maybe your child can accompany the dancing and singing with the guitar for a verse or two!

More Lyrics

The farmer takes a wife,
The farmer takes a wife,
Hi-ho, the derry-o,
The farmer takes a wife.

The wife takes a child,
The wife takes a child,
Hi-ho, the derry-o,
The wife takes a child.

The child takes a nurse,
The child takes a nurse,
Hi-ho, the derry-o,
The child takes a nurse.

The nurse takes a cow,
The nurse takes a cow,
Hi-ho, the derry-o,
The nurse takes a cow.

The cow takes a dog,
The cow takes a dog,
Hi-ho, the derry-o,
The cow takes a dog.

The dog takes a cat,
The dog takes a cat,
Hi-ho, the derry-o,
The dog takes a cat.

The cat takes a rat,
The cat takes a rat,
Hi-ho, the derry-o,
The cat takes a rat.

The rat takes the cheese,
The rat takes the cheese,
Hi-ho, the derry-o,
The rat takes the cheese.

The cheese stands alone,
The cheese stands alone,
Hi-ho, the derry-o,
The cheese stands alone.

The Farmer in the Dell

Track 55

The far - mer in the dell, the far - mer in the dell. Hi! Ho! The dai - ry - o, the far - mer in the dell.

B.I.N.G.O.

First published in 1780, this song is also known as "Bingo Was His Name-O." The song involves spelling the name of a dog over and over, increasing three number of letters replaced with handclaps each time, until the whole name is clapped, not sung. Bingo is also a popular game of chance, which is humorously depicted on the next page (being played by dogs, of course!).

Introducing the Page

1. Except for the four-string C chords at the beginning and end, this song played entrely on the 6th, 5th, and 4th strings.

2. Draw your child's attention to the fermata (introduced on page 45) over the final four-string C chord. Remind him or her to give that chord song extra time.

3. Notice that one rhythm is repeated three times to make much of the song: half—half—quarter–quarter–half (♩ ♩ ♩ ♩ ♩).
   B - I - N - G - O

Practice Suggestions

1. It's fun to sing and clap this song in the traditional way: The first time, sing all of the letters of the dog's name, "B I N G O"! The second time, clap instead of singing "B," the third time, replace "B" and "I," the third time, replace "B," "I," and "N," etc.

2. By now, your child should be accustomed to a good routine: count and clap the rhythms; recite the note names, frets, and strings; use additive practice; slow and steady wins the race!

Notes:

B.I.N.G.O.

Track 56

C

There was a far-mer had a dog, and Bin-go was his

name - o. B - I - N - G - O, B - I -

N - G - O, B - I - N - G - O, and Bin-go was his name - o.

C

Notes on the First String: Introducing High A

Just like ledger lines below the staff extend the staff lower, ledger lines above the staff extend the staff higher. The note one ledger line above the staff is called A.

Introducing the Page

1. Show your child the introduction to the A note on page 57. This new note is easy to recognize because it sits right above the high G that sits atop the staff.

2. This is the first note your child has learned that uses the 4th finger. Since that finger is smaller and not quite as strong as the other fingers, it will take some getting used to. Help them keep it a little curled and on its tip, right next to the fret; it is strongest this way. This will probably require careful attention to the angle of the hand to the neck; the palm of the hand should be parallel to the neck. Also, your child will need to *shift* his or her arm away from its usual position, toward the 5th fret. The 4th finger should not have to reach to find the 5th fret. The smaller you child's hand—the further they will have to shift to and from the A note.

3. Play the "High A Warm-up" together.

4. The song "Back to Russia" has an exotic, Russian sound. Listen to Track 59 on the recording to get familiar with the tune.

5. This song has four four-*bar* phrases. ("Bar" is another word for "measure.")

6. The first phrase is the first four bars. The next phrase, bars 5–8, is almost exactly the same, but an *octave* higher. We covered this term on page 82 of *Teach Your Child to Play Guitar, Book 1*. As you may recall, the shortest distance between two notes with the same name is an octave. It is always a distance of eight notes. The first phrase starts on low D. The second phrase sounds very similar but starts on high D.

7. Point out to your child the use of a fermata at the end of the third phrase. Give the C note extra time. In this case, the fermata just before the final phrase is being used to suspend time and create suspense.

Practice Suggestions

1. Make measures 5 and 6 into an exercise for your child to repeat several times before practicing the song. Going from the G on the 3rd fret of the 1st string up to the A and then back down to G requires moving both the fingers and the arm. This should be done very slowly at first.

2. Make measures 9 and 10 an exercise to repeat, as well.

3. The last measure should also become an exercise that is repeated.

Notes on the First String
Introducing High A

Just like ledger lines below the staff extend the staff lower, ledger lines above the staff extend the staff higher. The note one ledger line above the staff is called A. This A sounds higher than the other A's you've learned so far. To play high A, move your hand higher up the neck and use finger 4 to press the 1st string at the 5th fret.

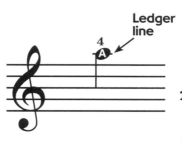

Track 58

High A Warm-up

Back to Russia

Track 59

Once up - on a time, long, long a - go, lived

Prin - cess An - a - sta - si - a   in a place called Rus - sia.

She was chased a - way from there,   ne - ver to re - turn back home.

Ma - ny hoped that she'd come back,   she'd come back to Rus - sia.

57

The Riddle Song

"The Riddle Song" is a 15th century English folk song which was carried by settlers to the American Appalachian region. It is one of many riddle songs from old England. This one was popularized in America by Burl Ives in the 1940s, on his debut album.

Introducing the Page

1. This beautiful melody provides a great chance for your child to practice playing the high A on string 1.

2. Except for strumming some four-string chords, this song is played entirely on the first three strings.

3. Notice that the second and third lines of the song are identical.

4. The quarter-note/half-note/quarter-note rhythm (♩ ♩ ♩) is an important feature of this song.

Practice Suggestions

1. Measures 6 and 7 should be repeated like an exercise as preparation for learning the song. This will give your child more practice shifting on the first string from G with the 3rd finger to A with the 4th finger, and back.

2. The last two measures require switching between plucking single notes and struming four-string chords. It would be a good idea to make these two measures an exercise, as well.

3. Be sure to practice counting and clapping the rhythm with your child until the quarter-note/half-note/quarter-note rhythm (♩ ♩ ♩) is mastered.

Subsequent Lessons

Identifying the new and/or challenging features of every new song, then isolating them as exercises and mastering them, should become a standard part of your child's approach to learning the guitar. Encourage him or her to be on the lookout for these important preparation opportunities!

Notes:

The Riddle Song

Track 60

C

Gave my love a cher - ry that has no stone. I

G

gave my love a chick - en that has no bone. I

gave my love a ring—— that has no end. I

C   **G⁷**   **C**

gave my love a ba - by that's not cry - in'.

Pickup Measures

Not all pieces of music begin on the first beat. Sometimes music begins with just part of a measure, which is called a *pickup*. Whatever portion of a measure is used in the pickup measure is subtracted from the last measure, which is then called an *incomplete measure*.

Introducing the Page

1. Explain to your child how the pickup and incomplete measure are like a pumpkin pie, with some slices in the pickup, and the rest in the ending, incomplete measure. Our pals, the alligator, cat, and dog will help!

2. Together with your child, practice the "Clap and Count out Loud" example. Point out that although it is in $\frac{4}{4}$ time, since the pickup has one beat, the last measure only has three. Learning the guitar will help your child with his or her arithmetic!

Practice Suggestions

1. Discuss with your child how this concept applies to "A-Tisket, A-Tasket." This song starts on the fourth beat of the pickup measure, so the last measure has only beats 1, 2, and 3.

2. The pickup and first two bars should be used as a preparation exercise and repeated several times.

Notes:

Pickup Measures

Not all pieces of music begin on the first beat. Sometimes music begins with just part of a measure, which is called a *pickup*.

A pickup is like a pumpkin pie. If you were to cut the pie into four equal pieces and take one piece away, there would be three pieces left. If you are playing in 4/4 time and the pickup measure has one quarter note, there will be three quarter notes in the last measure.

Playing in 3/4 time is like cutting the pie into three equal pieces: if there is one quarter note as a pickup, there will be two quarter notes in the last measure.

Clap and Count out Loud Track 61

Count: (1 2 3) 4   1 2 3 4   1 2 3 4   1 2 3 4   1 2 3 (4)

A-Tisket, A-Tasket

Track 62

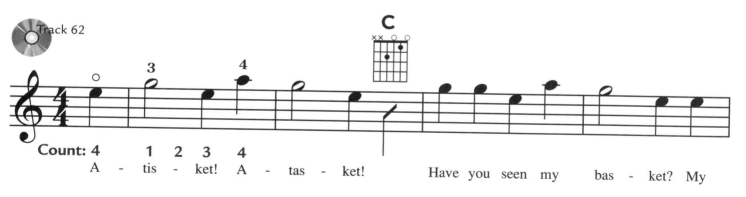

Count: 4   1 2 3 4

A - tis - ket! A - tas - ket!   Have you seen my   bas - ket? My

moth - er sent me   to the mar - ket,   on the way I   lost   it.

1 2 3 4   1 2 3

Parent Guide

The Yellow Rose of Texas

"The Yellow Rose of Texas" is a traditional folk song that begins with two quarter-note pickups on beats 3 and 4. Thus, the last measure of song has only two beats.

Introducing the Page

1. Point out the two pickup notes at the beginning. Explain that you'll be counting "1 2 3 4," and your child should start playing on beat 3.

2. Explain that, because the pickup measure has two beats, there are only two beats in the last measure and together, they equal one full four-beat measure!

3. This song is played entirely on the top four strings.

4. The third line is almost exactly like the first line. See if your child can spot the differences. Hint: in the first line, the second measure has a half note in the second full measure; in the third line, there are two quarter notes instead. Also, in the first line there is a chord strum on beat 3 of the fourth measure; in the third line, there is a plucked G-note, instead.

Practice Suggestions

1. When there are pickup notes, it is helpful to add an additional measure of counting before playing. For this song, try counting "1 2 3 4, 1 2" before playing. This will help ensure a solid tempo.

2. In the fourth complete measure (on the word "true"), it's a good idea to prepare the left-hand fingers on the C chord during the E half note. Make measures 3 and 4 an exercise to repeat.

Subsequent Lessons

Thinking ahead about finger movements, as suggested above in number 2 under Practice Suggestions, is an important part of good technical development on the guitar. Together, you and your child should always be looking for opportunities to be making "game plans" for the fingers. Think of the fingers as being members of a ball team, or dancers in a ballet. In both cases, either the coach or the choreographer is telling everyone what to do in advance. There's a plan! It should be the same with the fingers. It makes it so much easier to play the guitar!

Notes:

The Yellow Rose of Texas

Track 63

C

Count: 3   4   1   2   3   4

She's my   Rose-bud, she's my   darl-in'!   My   love   is   sweet   and   true!   I

still   can   hear   her   laugh-ter   'neath   Tex - as   skies   of   blue.   So   I'm

get - tin'   set   to   hur - ry   back   and   I   know   there   she'll   be,   my   sweet

Yel - low   Rose   of   Tex - as,   there   a - wait - in'   faith - ful - ly.

Tempo Signs

A *tempo sign* tells you how fast to play the music. The terms used describe the tempo or speed of music are from the Italian language, which is the universal language for all things musical.

Introducing the Page

1. *Andante* indicates a slow, walking pace.

2. *Moderato* means a moderate pace, neither slow nor fast.

3. *Allegro* literally translated mean lively. In music, we use it to describe a fast tempo.

4. "Three Tempo Rock" is very easy to play, so it will be no problem to perform it at three different tompos.

5. This song alternates between the 2nd finger and open strings.

Practice Suggestions

1. If your child can play the first measure of each line, they are ready to play the whole piece! Spend some time on each of those three measures, and it's time to play the song!

Notes:

Tempo Signs

A *tempo sign* tells you how fast to play the music. Below are the three most common tempo signs.

Andante ("ahn-DAHN-teh") **slow**

Moderato ("moh-deh-RAH-toh") **moderately**

Allegro ("ah-LAY-groh") **fast**

Three-Tempo Rock

Play three times: first time **Andante**, second time **Moderato**, third time **Allegro**.

Andante Track 64   **Moderato** Track 65   **Allegro** Track 66

1812 Overture

This piece was written in 1880 by the Russian composer Pyotr Ilyich Tchaikovsky to commemorate Russia's successful defense of its motherland against Napoleon's invasion in 1812. It has become a traditional accompaniment to fireworks displays in the United States during Fourth of July celebrations, often including actual cannons!

Introducing the Page

1. Point out that the first and second phrases, lines 1 and 2, are identical.

2. Point out that on the third line, finger 3 goes between the D-note on the 3rd fret of the 2nd string, and the F-note on the 3rd fret of the 4th string, while the 3rd-string A-note is being played with finger 2. Your child can have fun thinking of it as finger 3 jumping over finger 2 to go back and forth between the D- and F-notes. It's important they not just pick the 3rd finger up away from the notes; rather, the finger should move directly from one string to the next while the 2nd finger remains down on the 3rd string. The finger does not have to jump very high to get over the 3rd string…it's more like a little hop.

3. Point out to your child that the first, second, and fourth lines of the song can be played leaving the fingers down on the four-string C chord the whole time. In the first eight measures, lines 1 and 2, they need only add finger 3 to the D-note several times, but the other fingers can remain in position. It may feel awkward at first, but in the end this will make it easier to play the song.

Practice Suggestions

1. Make an exercise from the first two measures and repeat it many times. This will help your child get used to the idea of adding the 3rd finger to the four-string C chord fingering to play the D-notes.

2. Make an exercise of the second measure of line 3. This will help your child learn how to hop over the 3rd string with finger 3, while finger 2 remains down on the 3rd string.

3. Although "The 1812 Overture" should ultimately be played Allegro, initial practice should be very slow. Remember! Slow and steady wins the race!

Subsequent Lessons

This song is an excellent opportunity to stress the importance of planning out the finger movements in advance, and guiding fingers through their choreography, or game plan. Continue to make this a theme in your practice sessions and lessons.

1812 Overture

Track 67

C

Allegro

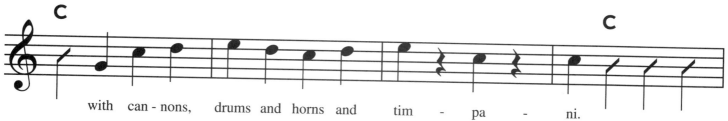

Tchai - kov - sky's   o - ver - ture   is   ex - plo - sive

C

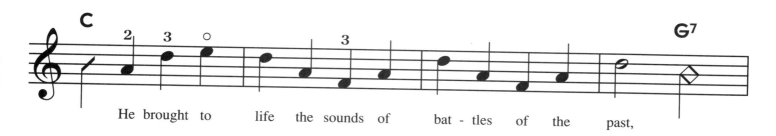

with can - nons,   drums and horns and   tim - pa - ni.

C   G7

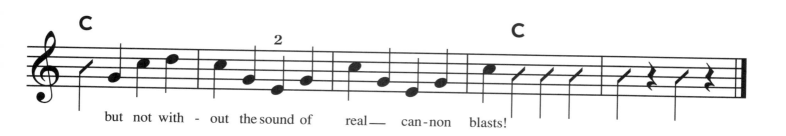

He brought to   life   the sounds of   bat - tles   of   the   past,

C   C

but not with - out the sound of   real — can - non blasts!

Reading Three-String Chords as Notes

So far, your child has been reading chords as slash chords, sometimes with chord diagrams above them. In this lesson they will learn to read chords as notes in the music.

Introducing the Page

1. Draw your child's attention to the chord diagram and photograph of the C chord fingering while litening to the chord being played on the recording.

2. Together with your child, look at the music to the right of the photograph and name the notes out loud, from the bottom note up, like this "G, C, E."

3. While looking at that music, they should strum the C chord.

4. Do the same procedure for the G chord and the G7 chord.

5. *Carmen* is an opera in four acts by the French composer Georges Bizet. "Theme from Carmen" is a famous theme from that opera, and it has two eight-measure phrases which are very similar. In fact, the first six measures are repeated exactly starting in measure 9. Measures 7 and 8 move to the G7 chord, and the last two measures of the piece move to a final C chord, which is the difference between the two phrases.

Practice Suggestions

1. Use additive practice.

2. Slow and steady wins the race!

3. Encourage your child to always be thinking ahead about finger movements. When they pick up a finger from a note, where is it going? A guitar student should always know!

Notes:

Reading Three-String Chords as Notes

Up until now, you have been reading chords as slash notes. When you play a chord, you simply play three or more notes at the same time. Chords can also be shown as notes in the music.
Here are some three-string chords you already know, shown as chords and as notes.

 Track 68

The Three-String C Chord

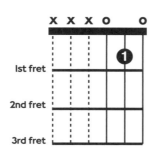

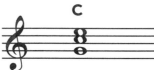

Here is the chord shown as notes.

 Track 69

The Three-String G Chord

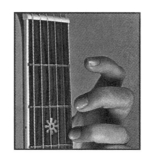

Here is the chord shown as notes.

 Track 70

The Three-String G⁷ Chord

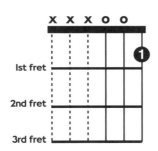

Here is the chord shown as notes.

Theme from Carmen Track 71

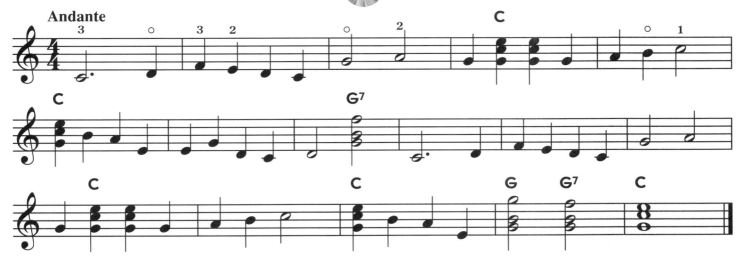

Reading Four-String Chords as Notes

In this lesson, we apply the skills learned for the three-string chords on page 69. Think how far your child has progressed—they will now be reading four notes at the same time!

Introducing the Page

1. Follow the same procedure you used for learning to read the three-string chords: together with your child by looking at the diagram and photo as you listen to the chord on the recording; then study the music to the right of the photograph and have your child recite the note names of the chord out loud from the bottom up. Do this for all three chords.

2. "Rockin' with Chords" uses all three chords on this page combined with a few plucked notes and some quarter rests.

3. Together with your child, make some observations about how the written music for each four-note chord looks; they do look different from one another. The C chord is contained within the staff—all of its notes are on a line or space. The G chord has a note sitting below the lowest line of the staff, and another sitting above the highest note of the staff. It looks very different from the C chord! The G7 chord has only one note outside the staff; the lowest note is just below the lowest line.

4. Because each chord looks different from the others, your child doesn't actually need to read each note of each chord. Rather, they can learn to recognize the chords and discern between them by perceiving their important features. Also, guitar music usually provides a chord symbol above the staff, which makes reading the chords easy.

Practice Suggestions

1. Pay special attention to the rests. Make an exercise of measure 10 and repeat it. Practice laying the right side of the right hand (the pinky side) across all six strings to stop them from ringing. Remind your child that a rest means SILENCE. There should be no string ringing during a rest.

2. As always, strive for slow, accurate practice. Confidence and ease will come quickly that way.

Notes:

Reading Four-String Chords as Notes

Here are the four-string versions of the chords on the previous page, shown as chords and as notes.

Track 72

The Four-String C Chord

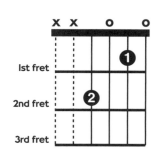 

Here is the chord shown as notes.

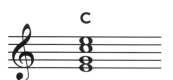

Track 73

The Four-String G Chord

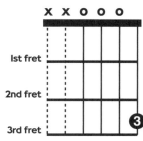 

Here is the chord shown as notes.

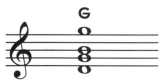

Track 74

The Four-String G⁷ Chord

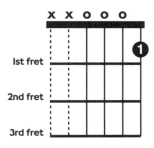 

Here is the chord shown as notes.

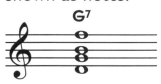

Rockin' with Chords
Track 75

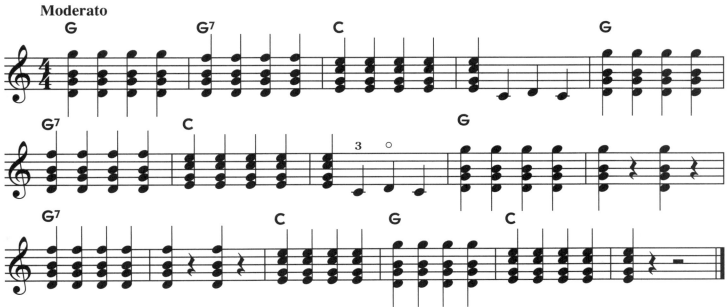

71

Bass-Chord Accompaniment

Now that your child can read chords as notes, they can create more interesting chord accompaniments by breaking up the chords, first playing the lowest note, called the *bass note*, then playing the rest of the notes. We call this *bass-chord accompaniment*. There are two standard types of bass-chord accompaniments in 4/4 time.

Introducing the Page

1. First, together with your child, review the four-string C chord. Then, keeping both fingers 2 and 1 on their C-chord frets, try playing just the lowest note (E on the 2nd fret, 4th string), and then strumming the rest of the strings (3rd, 2nd, and 1st strings).

2. Now, have your child prepare for the four-string G chord by placing finger 3 on the 3rd fret of the 1st string. First, pluck the bass note (low D on the open 4th string), then strum the rest of the strings in the chord (3rd, 2nd, and 1st strings).

3. Together with your child, play "Bass-Chord-Chord-Chord." It's important to notice that, for the C chord, you can place the 2nd finger first, and as you play it, you can add the finger 1 to the C note on the 1st fret of the 2nd string, keeping the 2nd finger down. Although guitar music often does not show it, the E note on the 4th string rings throughout the entire measure as you strum the upper three strings of the chord.

4. "Bass-Chord-Bass-Chord" uses C and G7. In this style of bass-chord accompaniment, we play the bass note and then strum only once, going back and forth between bass and strum.

Practice Suggestions

1. Pay special attention to the timing of the left-hand finger movements. Plucking the bass note first gives your child more time to place a finger or fingers on the other notes of a chord.

2. Combining plucks and strums may require watching the right hand, at first, but you should encourage your child to keep his or her eyes on the music as much of the time as possible.

Notes:

Bass-Chord Accompaniment

Now that you can read chords as notes, you can break them up by playing the lowest note of the chord, called the *bass note,* followed by the rest of the notes. We call this *bass-chord accompaniment.* There are two standard types of bass-chord accompaniments in $\frac{4}{4}$ time.

Bass-Chord-Chord-Chord Track 76

The first kind of bass-chord accompaniment is called *bass-chord-chord-chord* accompaniment. To play it, play the bass note once followed by the rest of the notes three times.

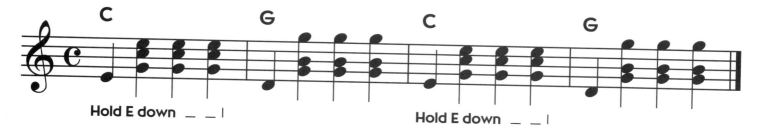

Bass-Chord-Bass-Chord Track 77

The other type of bass-chord accompaniment in $\frac{4}{4}$ time is called *bass-chord-bass-chord* accompaniment. To play it, play the bass note once followed by the rest of the notes one time, and repeat the bass note followed by the rest of the notes again.

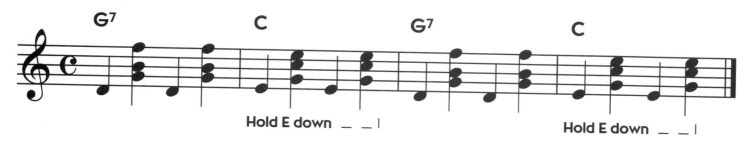

Can-Can (duet)

"Can-Can" is from a melody called *The Infernal Galop* by Jacques Offenbach, which is traditionally associated with a high-energy, physcially demanding dance called the *can-can* from 19th century France. This is a special lesson because, if you wish, you and your child can play a duet! If you prefer, your child can play along with the recording or someone else.

Introducing the Page

1. Point out that Part 1, the accompaniment part, is in the bass-chord-chord-chord style and uses the four-string C and G7 chords.

2. Part 1 has two four-string chords strummed in the next-to-last measure.

3. Your child should also learn to play Part 2, the melody, so you can switch parts when playing the duet.

Practice Suggestions

1. First, have your child learn and master Part 1, the accompaniment part.

2. To learn Part 1, have your child make an exercise of the next-to-last measure and repeat it until it is easy.

3. Part 2 includes the high A on the 5th fret of the 1st string. Remind your child to shift the hand and arm up the neck to get finger 4 to the 5th fret, for that note, and then shift back. Make measure 4 into an exercise to repeat, and measures 7–8. Mastering these measures will prepare your child to play Part 2 with confidence.

Subsequent Lessons

When playing a duet, it is very important for the two parts to be exactly together. It's a good idea for you both to count out loud, and listen to how well your parts are fitting together. When two guitars play EXACTLY together, it is hard to tell there are two!

Notes:

Can-Can (duet)

Track 78

"Can-Can" is a *duet*, which means there are two versions of music that are played at the same time. Part 1 is the *accompaniment* part. Play it slowly at first, and work out all the chords. Once you can play it without stopping, have your parent, teacher, or a friend play along with Part 2, the melody part, which is at the bottom of the page. You can also play along with the Recording. Once you have played the duet a few times, switch parts and play the melody while someone else plays the accompaniment.

Part 1: Accompaniment Track 79

Allegro

Hold E down _ _ _ ⌐   Hold E down _ _ _ _ _ _ _ _ _ _ _ _ ⌐

Hold E down _ _ _ _ _ ⌐

Hold E down _ _ _ _ ⌐   Hold E down _ _ _ _ _ _ _ _ _ ⌐

Hold E down _ _ ⌐   Hold E _ _ _ ⌐
                            down

Hold E _ _ _ _ ⌐
down

Part 2: Melody Track 80

Allegro

Dynamics

Music is much more interesting when there are variations in how loud or soft it is played. Symbols that show how loud or soft to play are called *dynamics*. Like the tempos covered on page 65, the names for the dynamics come from Italian, the universal language of music.

Introducing the Page

1. Explain the symbols, pronunciation, meaning of the dynamics symbols shown on page 77.

2. Together with your child, look through "Theme from Beethoven's Fifth Symphony" and note all of the dynamics.

3. Also, look for fermatas (⌢, page 45). Remind your child that this symbol means to pause and add extra time to the note. This is either done at the end of the piece to add a feeling of finality, or in the middle, to suspend time and create drama.

4. Point out the double stops, where two notes are stacked (page 23), like a two-note chord. There's one on the fourth line, measure 2, and in the next-to-last measure.

5. Point out that the most important feature of this melody is three repeated notes followed by a small skip down to a lower note. This is one of the world's most famous tunes!

Practice Suggestions

1. Encourage your child to experiment with *forte* versus *piano*. How loud is loud enough? Make sure your child doesn't pluck the string too hard; it could break! And remember, there is a *fortissimo* on the last line, which is even louder! How soft is soft enough? If we play too soft, no one can hear us! Finding the right volume takes practice.

2. Although this piece should be played at a fast, *Allegro* tempo once learned, initial practice should be slow and careful.

Subsequent Lessons

By now, it should be a habit for your child to always review the music for a new song and look for its special features. Now, they can add dynamics to the list of things to look for.

Notes:

Dynamics

Symbols that show how loud or soft to play are called *dynamics*.
These symbols come from Italian words. Four of the most
common dynamics are shown here.

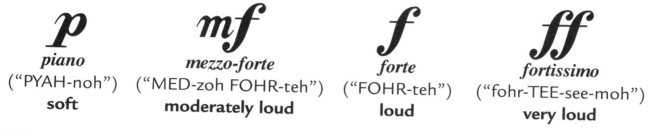

Theme from Beethoven's Fifth Symphony

Introducing the Whole Rest

A *whole rest* indicates a full measure of rest (silence). This lesson provides another opportunity for you to play a duet with your child, or for him or her to play a duet with the guitar on the recording for this book. This time, the two parts are connected in one *score*, instead of in two different parts, like "Can-Can" on page 75.

Introducing the Page

1. Point out the whole rest lesson on page 79, explaining that when the whole rest symbol appears on the staff, it means one measure of silence. Together, count out loud and clap the rhythm in "Clap and Count out Loud."

2. Explain how the duet score for "The Desert Song" works: When you play Part 1 of the duet, only play the music on the staff labeled number 1. When you play Part 2, just play the music on the staff labeled number 2.

3. Together with your child, look through "The Desert Song," notice all of the dynamics, and find the whole rest. It's in Part 1 on the second line, measure 4. Also, point out the pickup measure has three beats, so the final measure has only one beat.

4. Together, count out loud and clap the rhythms for Part 1.

5. Then, do the same for Part 2.

6. Now, you clap Part 1, and have your child clap Part 2.

7. Finally, switch parts.

8. "Echo Rock" is a fun song to play because the dynamics create an echo effect. Musicians sometimes think of dynamics as creating a sense of near (*forte*) or far (*piano*). Your child can imagine playing the first measure *forte*, and having the sound bounce back from a far off mountain, *piano*.

Practice Suggestions

1. Use additive practice.

2. Slow and steady wins the race.

Notes:

Introducing the Whole Rest

Rest for a whole measure.

Clap and Count out Loud

Count: 1 2 3 4   (1 2 3 4)   1 2 3 4   (1 2 3 4)

The Desert Song (duet)

Part 1   **Part 2**

Like "Can-Can" on page 132, "The Desert Song" is a duet. This time, Part 1 is written directly above Part 2. When you play Part 1 of the duet, only play the music on the staff labeled number 1. When you play Part 2, just play the music on the staff labeled number 2.

Echo Rock

Ties

A *tie* is a curved line that connects two notes of the same pitch. The time of the second note is added to that of the first. For example, a whole note (four beats) tied to a quarter note (one beat) equals five beats.

Introducing the Page

1. Show your child the examples at the top of page 81. Explain how these examples show that a tie is how notes are written when they last longer than the time left in a measure. For example, in common time (**C**), there are only four beats in a measure, so the only way to write a note that lasts for five beats is tie a whole note to a quarter note in the next measure, or tie a dotted half note to a half note like measures 7 and 8.

2. Together with your child, practice "Clap and Count out Loud" until the ties are easy to read and perform.

3. Point out that "Shenandoah" has a half-note pickup, played on beats 3 and 4 before the first complete measure of the song. Because of this, the last measure of the song is incomplete and has only beats 1 and 2.

4. Together, look through "Shenandoah" for all of its other special features. First, point out all of the ties. Then notice the tempo marking is *Moderato*, which means moderate, so the song is neither fast nor slow. There are dynamics written above the music (because the lyrics are written below). You'll see the piece begins *mezzo forte*, moderately loud, then it changes to *piano*, soft, back to *mezzo forte*, and it ends *forte*, loud. The last note of the song has a *fermata* written above it, so hold that note longer than its written value (it's a half note, which is two beats, so hold it for four beats).

Practice Suggestions

1. Together, count out loud and clap the rhythms for "Shenandoah."

2. Slow and steady wins the race.

3. The song has four phrases, all starting on beat 3 of a measure, on the words "Oh" (the beginning), "Way" (measure 4) "Oh" (measure 8) and "Way" (measure 12). Practice one phrase at a time until mastered, using additive practice: Master the first phrase, then the second, then the first and second together, then the third, then the first, second and third together, etc.

Notes:

Ties

A *tie* is a curved line that connects two of the same note. When two notes are tied, don't play the second note, but keep the first note playing until the second note is done. You are really adding the two notes together.

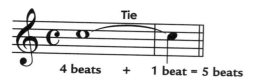

4 beats   +   1 beat = 5 beats

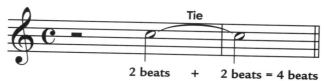

2 beats   +   2 beats = 4 beats

Clap and Count out Loud Track 87

Count: 1   2   3   4   1   2   3   4   1   2   3   4   1   2   3   4

Shenandoah Track 88

Moderato

Oh,   Shen - an - doah, _____ I   long   to   hear   you. _____   Way ___

hey, _____ you   rol - ling   riv - er! _____ Oh,   Shen - an - doah, ___

___ I   long   to   hear   you. _____ Way   hey, _____ we're   bound   a -

way _____ a - cross   the   wide   Mis - sou - ri.

When the Saints Go Marching In (duet)

Now you can play this fun song in a duet with your child, or, they can play a duet with the guitar on the recording for this book. The two parts are connected in one score like "The Desert Song." Your child should learn to play both parts but it's a good idea for them to play Part 1 first, because it will be good practice reading and playing ties.

Introducing the Page

1. Point out all of the ties in Part 1. There are four of them.

2. Notice that the piece begins on beat 2 of a three-beat pickup measure, so there is a one-beat incomplete measure at the end.

3. Notice the tempo marking and the dynamics.

4. Point out that Part 2 of "When the Saints Go Marching In" starts with rests. Part 1 plays the beginning of the melody alone, then Part 2 comes in on beat 2 of the first complete measure, *imitating* the melody down on the bass strings. It's as if the two parts are having a conversation!

5. When it's time for your child to learn Part 2, point out the two-string, three-string, and four-string chords.

Practice Suggestions

1. Together, count out loud and clap the rhythms for Part 1 of "When the Saints Go Marching In."

2. Together, count out loud and clap the rhythms for Part 2.

3. Now, have your child clap Part 1 while you clap part 2. Both of you should be counting out loud. Then, switch the parts you are clapping.

4. The song is written on four lines of music. Have your child practice one line at a time, always including the first note of the next line. This should be done in an additive fashion: line 1 + one note, line 2 + one note, then lines one and two together + one note, etc.

Notes:

When the Saints Go Marching In (duet)

Part 1 Track 90

Part 2 Track 91

Review: Music Matching Games

Chords

Draw a line to match each chord frame on the left to the correct notation on the right.

1.

2.

3.

4.

5.

6.

Symbols

Draw a line to match each symbol on the left to its name or definition on the right.

1.   Dotted half note

2.   Whole rest

3. $\frac{3}{4}$ Half-note slash

4.   Dotted-half-note slash

5. $f\!f$ Tie

6.   Three beats in a measure

7. Moderato   Fermata

8.   Common time

9. $m\!f$ Loud

10. $\mathbf{C}$ Moderately loud

11. Allegro   Soft

12. p Very loud

13. Andante   Slow

14.   Moderately

15. f Fast

Notes

Draw a line to match each note on the left to its correct notation on the right.

1.

2.

3.

4.

5.

6.

7.

8.

9.

10.

Answer Key

Chords
1: page 69; 2: page 69; 3: page 69; 4: page 71
5: page 71; 6: page 71

Symbols
1: page 7; 2: page 81; 3: page 21; 4: page 21;
5: page 75; 6: page 79; 7: page 65; 8: page 37;
9: page 75; 10: page 15; 11: page 15; 12: page 75
13: page 65; 14: page 45; 15: page 75

Notes
1: page 41; 2: page 25; 3: page 5; 4: page 45;
5: page 49; 6: page 29; 7: page 33; 8: page 13
9: page 17; 10: page 25

Fingerboard Chart

STRINGS

6th	5th	4th	3rd	2nd	1st
E	A	D	G	B	E

FRETS	

← Open →

← 1st Fret →

← 2nd Fret →

← 3rd Fret →

← 5th Fret →

STRINGS

6th	5th	4th	3rd	2nd	1st
E	A	D	G	B	E
F				C	F
	B	E	A		
G	C	F		D	G
					A

Fingerboard diagram

6th	5th	4th	3rd	2nd	1st
E	A	D	G	B	E
F				C	F
	B	E	A		
G	C	F		D	G
					A

Chord Encyclopedia

Here are all the chords you know.

The three-string C chord
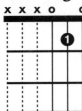

The three-string G chord
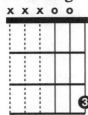

The three-string G⁷ chord
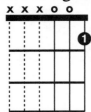

The three-string D⁷ chord
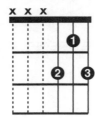

The four-string C chord
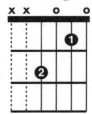

The four-string G chord
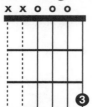

The four-string G⁷ chord
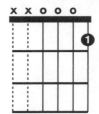

Notes

Certificate of Promotion

This certifies that

_____

has mastered and perfected

Alfred's Teach Your Child To Play Guitar 2

_____
Teacher / Parent

_____
Date